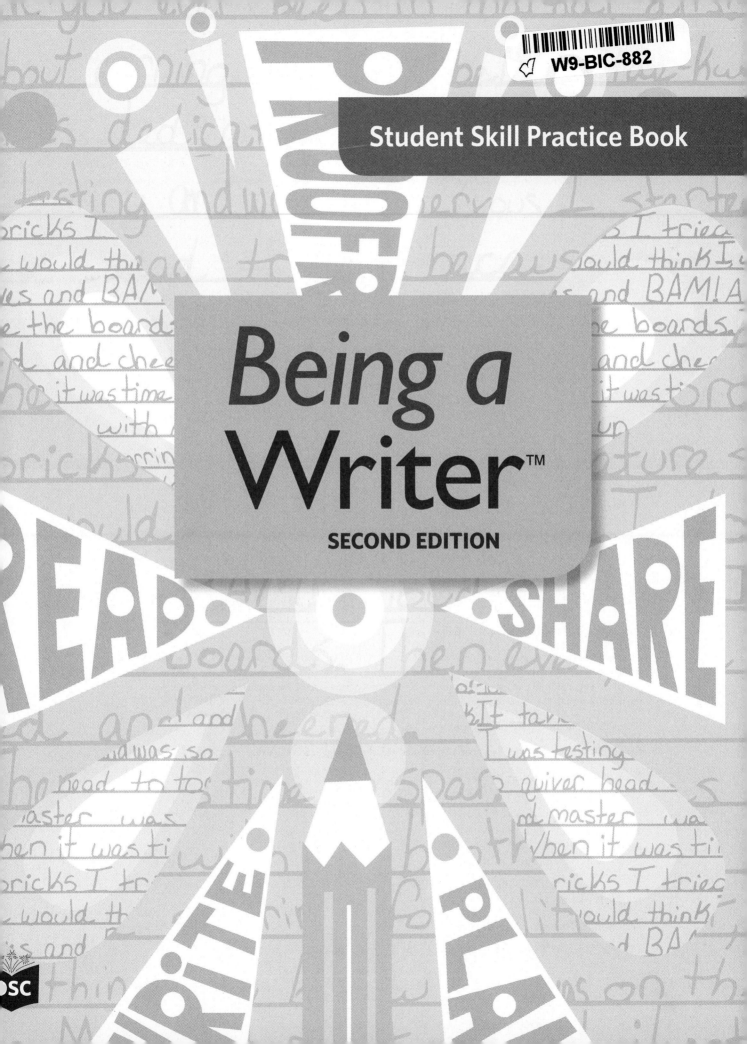

Student Skill Practice Book

Being a
Writer™

SECOND EDITION

First edition published 2007. Second edition 2014.

Being a Writer and DSC ClassView are trademarks of Developmental Studies Center.

Cover illustration by Michael Wertz
Illustrations by Nancy Meyers and Rick Brown

Developmental Studies Center
1250 53rd Street, Suite 3
Emeryville, CA 94606-2965
(800) 666-7270; fax: (510) 464-3670
devstu.org

ISBN 978-1-61003-263-6

Printed in the United States of America

1 2 3 4 5 6 7 8 9 10 EBM 23 22 21 20 19 18 17 16 15 14

CONTENTS

(continues)

CONTENTS (continued)

Jim's Puppy

A. Read the sentences. Circle the words that tell who the sentences are about.

1. Jim wakes up early.

2. The puppy is barking.

3. Mom comes into the room.

B. Read the sentences. Draw a line under the words that tell what happens.

1. The puppy cries.

2. Jim picks her up.

3. He pets her soft fur.

C. Write a sentence that tells about the picture.

Jim is eating with the puppy.

My Kitten

A. Complete each sentence. Write the word that tells who or what the sentence is about.

bowl   milk   kitten

1. The _____kitten_____ jumps up.

2. The _____rbowl_____ tips over.

3. The _____milk_____ spills.

B. Look at each picture. Write the word that tells what the kitten does.

sleeps   plays   drinks

1.   The kitten _____drinks_____.

2.   The kitten _____plays_____.

3.   The kitten _____sleeps_____.

C. Write a sentence telling about a dog or a cat.

Summer Fun

A. Draw a line from the picture to the matching sentence. Circle the naming part. Put a box around the telling part.

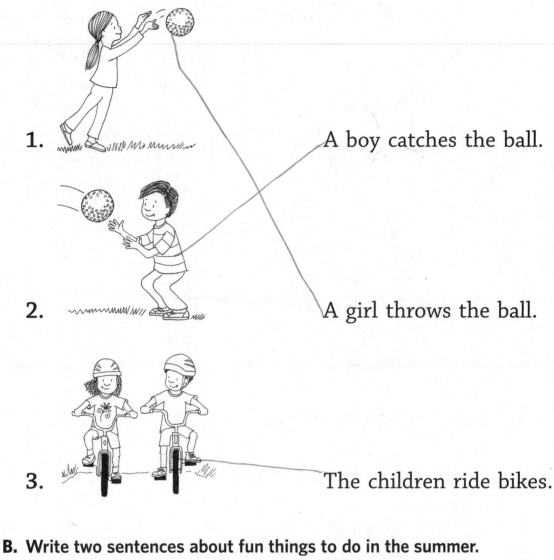

1. A boy catches the ball.

2. A girl throws the ball.

3. The children ride bikes.

B. Write two sentences about fun things to do in the summer.

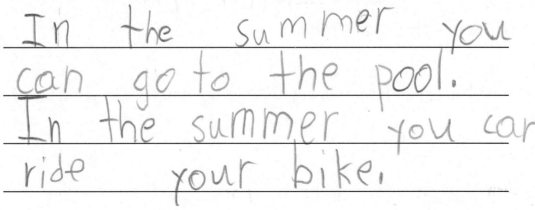

In the summer you can go to the pool. In the summer you can ride your bike.

On the Playground

A. Read each sentence. Circle the noun.

1. The playground is crowded.

2. The boy runs fast.

3. The swing can go high.

4. The seesaw goes up and down.

5. The girl is friendly.

6. Let's share a snack!

B. Choose a noun from this page. Write the noun. Draw a picture of it.

A Story for a Dog

A. Look at each picture. Complete each sentence with a noun that matches the picture.

pillow   dog   brother   ~~book~~   treat   ~~tail~~

1. I like this __book__.

2. I keep it under my __pillow__.

3. I read it to my __brother__.

4. I read it to my __dog__, too.

5. My dog wags her __tail__.

6. I give her a __treat__.

B. Choose a noun from this page. Use the noun to write a sentence.

My Friend and I

A. Read each sentence. Circle the noun.

1. Let's eat lunch.

2. We go to the lunchroom.

3. We sit at a table.

4. My friend giggles.

5. She eats a red apple.

6. I eat a mushy banana.

B. Make a list of your four favorite foods for lunch.

1. Milk

2. water

3. mak n and cheese

4. water melon

The Outdoors

A. Circle the word that matches the picture.

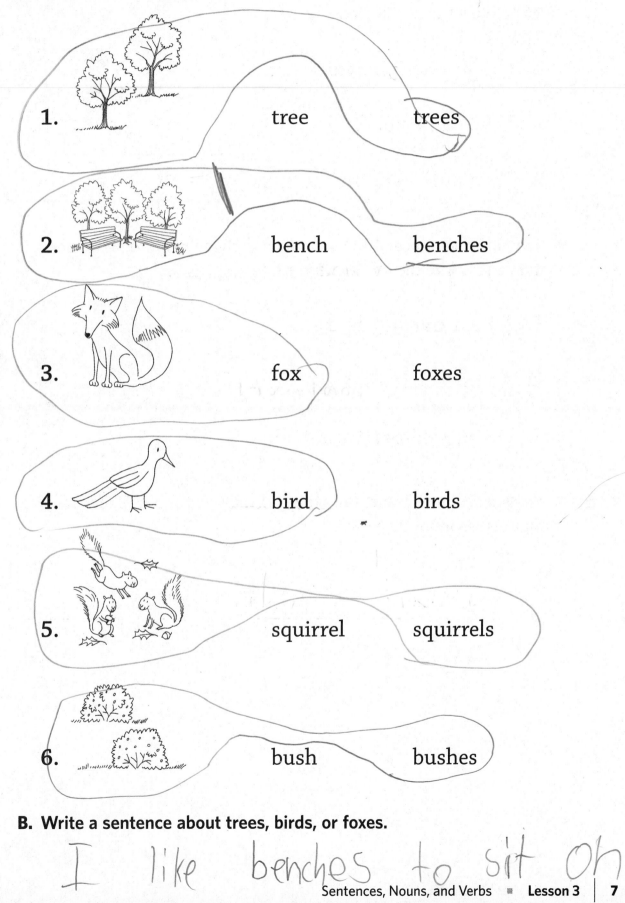

1. tree   trees

2. bench   benches

3. fox   foxes

4. bird   birds

5. squirrel   squirrels

6. bush   bushes

B. Write a sentence about trees, birds, or foxes.

I like benches to sit on.

A School Day

A. Read each sentence. Add _s_ to the noun to show more than one. Write the letter on the line.

1. The teacher_s_ work hard.

2. They gather book_s_.

3. They put them on the desk_s_.

B. Read each sentence. Add _es_ to the underlined noun to show more than one. Write the ending on the line.

1. We eat our <u>lunch</u>_es_.

2. We open juice <u>box</u>_es_.

3. The juice drips on our <u>dress</u>_es_.

C. Write a sentence about something in your classroom. Use a noun that names more than one.

I see Plants on the window sill.

The Porch

A. Read the story. Circle three mistakes with nouns that name more than one.

The house has a porch. Two doges nap. The pups drink from two dish. Two leashes lie nearby. Three boy play.

B. Read each sentence. Add *s* or *es* to the noun. Write the ending on the lines.

1. Two cat___ play.

2. They jump into box___.

3. They chase bird___.

C. Write a sentence about animals you like to draw. Use a noun that names more than one.

Play Ball

A. Draw a line from each picture to the verb that matches.

1.   hit

2.   blow

3.   run

B. Read each sentence. Circle the verb.

1. We play a game.

2. I hit the ball.

3. The children yell.

C. Choose a verb from this page. Write the verb. Draw a picture to show the action.

On the Playground

A. Look at each picture. Complete the sentence with a verb from the word box.

slide   talk   jump   swing   hide

1. The girls _____.

2. We _____.

3. Two children _____.

4. You _____.

5. I _____.

B. Choose a verb from this page. Use the verb to write a sentence.

Hide and Seek

A. Read each sentence. Circle the verb. Draw a line to the picture that tells about it.

1. You count to 10.

2. I hide under the bed.

3. You find me!

B. Complete each sentence. Use a verb from the word box.

| hide   play   look |

1. We _____ a game.

2. First, I _____ from you.

3. Then you _____ for me.

C. Write a sentence about playing a game.

Who Says That?

A. Look at each picture. Draw a line to the sentence that goes with it.

1. The chicks peep.

2. The chick peeps.

3. The hen clucks.

4. The hens cluck.

B. Look at each picture. Circle the sentence that goes with it.

1. The cow moos.

   The cows moos.

2. The ducks quacks.

   The ducks quack.

C. Choose a noun and a verb from this page. Use them to write a new sentence.

Who Does It?

A. Choose the correct word to complete each sentence.
Write the word on the line.

| stand   stands |

1. The cows _____.

| ride   rides |

2. The children _____.

| drive   drives |

3. The farmer _____.

| eat   eats |

4. The goat _____.

| drink   drinks |

5. The pigs _____.

| run   runs |

6. The dog _____.

B. Choose a noun and a verb from this page. Use them to write a new sentence.

What We Eat

A. Choose the correct word to complete each sentence. Write the word on the line.

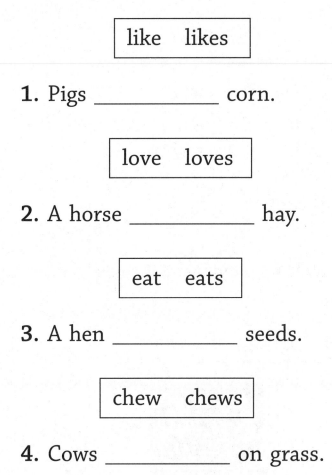

| like   likes |

1. Pigs _____ corn.

| love   loves |

2. A horse _____ hay.

| eat   eats |

3. A hen _____ seeds.

| chew   chews |

4. Cows _____ on grass.

B. Read the story. Look at each verb. Circle the verb if it does not match its noun.

The boys feeds the hens. The hens lays eggs.

Mom gets the eggs. Dad cook the eggs. The boys

eats the eggs.

C. Draw a picture of one or two animals. Write a sentence to tell about the picture.

Nighttime

A. Complete each sentence. Write the word that tells who or what the sentence is about.

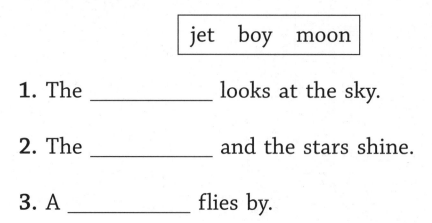

| jet | boy | moon |

1. The _____ looks at the sky.

2. The _____ and the stars shine.

3. A _____ flies by.

B. Complete each sentence. Write the word that tells what happens in the picture.

| sleeps | barks | shines |

1. A star _____.

2. A dog _____.

3. The boy _____.

C. Write a sentence about something you can see at night.

Up in the Sky

A. Circle the noun that matches each picture.

1. rainbow   rainbows

2. cloud   clouds

3. bush   bushes

B. Read each sentence. Add _s_ or _es_ to the noun. Write the endings on the lines.

1. We sit on park bench___.

2. We paint picture___ of clouds.

3. We use paintbrush___.

C. Choose a word that names more than one. Use it to write a sentence.

The Rain

A. Look at the picture. Complete each sentence with a verb from the word box.

hide   run   fall

1. Drops of rain _____.

2. The children _____ inside.

3. The dogs _____.

B. Choose the correct word to complete each sentence. Write the word on the line.

play   plays

1. The kids _____ in the puddles.

jump   jumps

2. One girl _____ over them.

C. Write another sentence about the picture on this page.

The Bus

A. Read each sentence. Write *T* (for telling sentence) or *A* (for asking sentence) on the line.

1. Pam rides the bus. ___

2. What color is the bus? ___

3. Where does the bus go? ___

4. The bus stops at the corner. ___

B. Draw a line under the sentence that is correct.

1. The bus has big wheels.

2. the bus is yellow?

C. Write a sentence that tells about a bus.

The Train

A. Write a period after each telling sentence. Write a question mark after each asking sentence.

   1. Sammy likes trains___

   2. The train goes fast___

   3. Where does the train stop___

B. Draw a line from each asking sentence to the picture that shows the answer.

   1. Who rides the train?

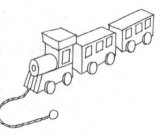

   2. Which train is big?

   3. Where is the toy train?

C. Write a question you have about trains.

Walk or Ride?

A. Read the sentences. Circle the two mistakes.

ted walks to school.

Who rides a bike to school.

B. Write sentences to answer the questions.

1. How do you get to school?

   _____

   _____

2. What do you take with you to school?

   _____

   _____

C. Write one telling sentence about walking. Write one asking sentence about riding.

A Trip to the Store

A. Read each sentence. Draw a line under the noun.

1. I went to the store.

2. My sister went, too.

3. We need shoes.

B. Read each sentence. Draw a line under the proper noun.

1. The Shoe Shack was full of people.

2. I saw my friend Gus there.

3. I saw my teacher, Miss Parker.

4. Everyone shops on Davis Street.

C. Write a sentence about a special friend you have.

The Bakery

A. Read each sentence. Write the underlined noun correctly.

1. My name is <u>rob</u>.

   _____

2. My sister's name is <u>ana</u>.

   _____

3. We live in <u>san jose</u>.

   _____

4. Our mom works at <u>bliss bakery</u>.

   _____

5. The bakery is on <u>front street</u>.

   _____

6. It is near <u>grant school</u>.

   _____

B. Write a sentence about the street where you live. Draw a picture to go with it.

About You

A. Read the story. Circle one mistake in each sentence.

I went to the market on doyle Street. My friend dan went with me. I got an Apple and a pear. Dan got some Milk.

B. Complete the sentences with proper nouns.

1. My full name is _____.

2. I have a friend named _____.

3. I would name a kitten _____.

4. I would name a puppy _____.

C. Write two sentences that tell more about you and a pet. Use one proper noun in each sentence.

Doing Chores

A. Read each sentence about today. Draw a line to the sentence that tells about the same action, only in the past.

1. Today Dad cooks.   Yesterday I cleaned.

2. Today I clean.   Yesterday Dad cooked.

3. Today Sari helps.   Yesterday Sari helped.

B. Read each pair of sentences. Draw a line under the sentence that is correct.

1. Yesterday Sam washed the pots.

   Right now Sam washed the pans.

2. Yesterday Mom works outside.

   Right now Mom works inside.

3. Yesterday I pick up my toys.

   Right now I pick up my socks.

C. Choose a verb from this page. Use it to write a sentence. Tell about something you did this week.

Making Soup

A. Choose the correct word to complete each sentence. Write the word on the line.

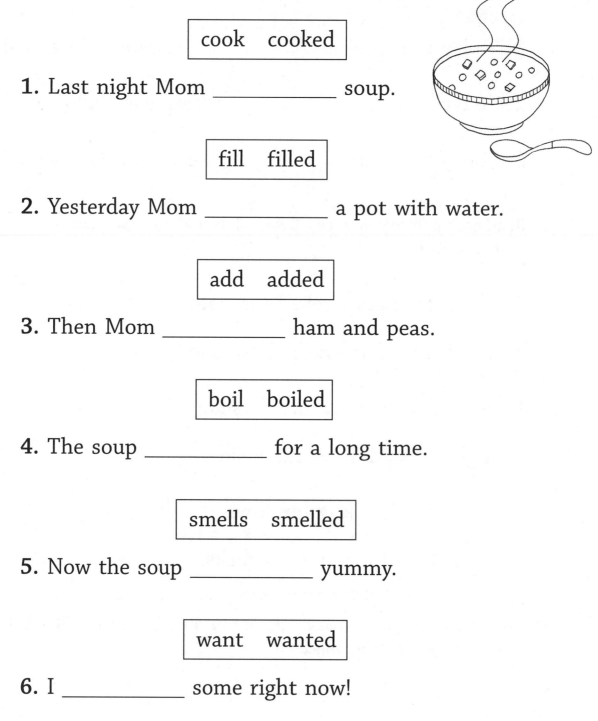

cook   cooked

1. Last night Mom _____ soup.

fill   filled

2. Yesterday Mom _____ a pot with water.

add   added

3. Then Mom _____ ham and peas.

boil   boiled

4. The soup _____ for a long time.

smells   smelled

5. Now the soup _____ yummy.

want   wanted

6. I _____ some right now!

B. Pretend you made soup yesterday. Write a sentence about it. Use one of these verbs: *cooked*, *added*, or *smelled*.

Clean Your Room!

A. Write each verb so that it tells about the past.

Now	In the Past
look	_____
smell	_____
work	_____
wash	_____

B. Read the story. Circle four verbs that do not correctly tell about the past.

Yesterday my room looks bad. Then I cleaned it. Dad help. We pickd up socks. We folded pants. We wash the floor. Now my room looks good.

C. Write a sentence to tell what your room looks like today. Then write a sentence to tell what it looked like yesterday.

Now or Later

A. Draw a line under the sentences that tell about the future.

1. Today we write. Tomorrow we will read.

2. Lewis paints now. Tomorrow he will draw.

3. The fair starts today. The fair will end in a week.

B. Read the story. Draw a line under the verbs that tell about the future.

The art room is a mess. We will clean it up. Some water spilled on my desk. I will get a cloth. I will wipe the desk with it. Our pictures are great! We will show them to everyone!

C. Write a sentence about something you will do tomorrow.

Follow the Leader

A. Complete the sentences. Use the verbs from the word box.

will play will go will lead

1. You g<u>o</u> first.

   Next time I _____ first.

2. You <u>lead</u> me.

   Later I _____ you.

3. We <u>play</u> together today.

   Tomorrow we _____ together again.

B. Choose the correct verb to complete each sentence. Write the verbs on the lines.

comes will come

1. Later today Ruby _____ to my house.

go will go

2. Tomorrow I _____ to her house.

sit will sit

3. Right now we _____ in class.

C. Write a sentence about something you will do with a friend.

At the Beach

A. Complete the sentences. Use the verbs from the word box.

> will eat   will rest   will set

1. Right now the sun shines.

   Later the sun _____.

2. The children play now.

   They _____ tonight.

3. The children are not hungry now.

   They _____ later.

B. Write three sentences about what the
people in the picture are going to do.

_____

_____

_____

_____

_____

C. Write a sentence about what you are doing right now. Then write a
sentence about what you will do later today.

The Dogs' Day Out

A. Draw a line under the sentences that show strong feeling.

1. Two dogs are in a park.

2. Wow, that thin dog is tall!

3. The little dog is so tiny!

4. His bark is really loud!

5. Is the big dog afraid?

6. Look, he is running away!

B. Write another sentence about the cartoon. Be sure the sentence shows a strong feeling.

Run, Bunny, Run

A. Add a period (.) or an exclamation point (!) at the end of each sentence.

1. A bunny is eating a white flower___

2. Oh no, a fox is coming___

3. The rabbit needs to run really fast___

4. Yay, the bunny is safe___

5. Wow, that fox is mad___

6. He will try again tomorrow___

B. Write a sentence that shows a strong feeling about an animal you like or do not like.

Elephant Jokes

A. Add a question mark (?) or an exclamation point (!) at the end of each sentence.

1. What do you call an elephant at the North Pole___

   I call it "lost"___

2. What do you get when you cross a potato with an elephant___

   You get mashed potatoes___

B. What if you opened your front door and saw an elephant? Write some sentences about it. Show strong feeling.

_____

_____

_____

In the Classroom

A. Read each sentence. Write *T* for telling sentence, *A* for asking sentence, or *S* for a sentence that shows strong feeling.

1. Do you have a pencil?   ___

2. The pencil is under the desk.   ___

3. I must find my pencil!   ___

B. Read each sentence. Write the missing end mark.

1. The book is on the shelf___

2. That is the best book I ever read___

3. What book are you reading___

C. Write about your favorite book. Write a telling sentence and a sentence that shows strong feeling.

My Aunt and Uncles

A. Read the sentences. Draw a line under each proper noun.

I have an aunt. Her name is Katrina. She lives in Dallas. It is a big city. Katrina has a big dog. She calls the dog Billy Boy.

B. Write each underlined noun correctly.

1. I have two <u>Uncles</u>. _____

2. Uncle Mike lives in <u>new york</u>. _____

3. The other uncle's name is <u>max</u>. _____

C. Write a sentence about someone in your family. Use a proper noun.

The United States

A. Choose the correct verb to complete each sentence. Write the verb on the line.

| will learn   learned |

1. Yesterday we _____ about Texas.

| will see   see |

2. Tomorrow we _____ a movie about Alaska.

| wanted   want |

3. Now I _____ a book about the

United States.

B. Complete the chart. Write the missing verbs.

Now	In the Past	In the Future
look	_____	will look
visit	visited	_____
_____	stayed	will stay

C. Write a sentence about a place you visited in the past. Then write a sentence about a place you will visit in the future.

The Morning

A. Read the sentences. Draw a line under each command.

1. Brush your teeth.

2. I wash my hands.

3. Comb your hair.

4. Put on your shoes.

5. My sister ties my shoes.

6. Find your backpack.

B. What should this boy do before he goes outside? Write two sentences telling him what to do.

_____

_____

_____

Clean Up, Please

A. Draw a line from each picture to the command that goes with it.

1.

Pick up your socks.

2.

Wash your hands.

3.

Open the window, please.

4.

Tie your shoe.

5.

Throw the paper away.

B. Write two commands that grown-ups might give children about cleaning up their rooms.

A Walk with Peppy

A. Circle the four mistakes in these sentences.

The dog needs a walk. find the leash. put

it on Peppy

Wait for Mom. wait for Sara. Now we

are ready.

B. Write each command correctly.

1. walk more slowly

_____

2. hold onto the leash

_____

C. Look at the picture. Write two commands that could go with it.

All Kinds of Animals

A. Read each sentence. Circle the word that shows belonging.

1. The monkey's tail is long.

2. The lamb's face is cute.

3. The bunny's fur is soft.

B. Add 's to show what each thing belongs to. Then draw a line from each thing to its picture.

1. the dog___ bowl

2. the bird___ nest

3. the bear___ nose

C. Write a sentence telling what a rabbit's ears or an elephant's trunk is like.

Around the House

A. Add **'s** to show that something belongs to the baby, to Dad, and to the boy.

1. The toy is in the baby___ crib.

2. The computer is on Dad___ desk.

3. The book is in the boy___ bedroom.

B. Choose the correct word to complete each sentence. Write the word on the line.

cat's   cats

1. The boy washes the _____ dish.

birds   bird's

2. Dora cleans the _____ cage.

dog's   dogs

3. Grandpa fills the _____ bowl.

C. Look at the picture. Whose bike has a flat tire? Write a sentence to answer the question.

Trouble with Clothes

A. Circle the three mistakes with words that show belonging.

Kim has a new stuffed bear. She loves the

bears eyes. They look like stars.

Kim brings the bear to her friends party.

Kims friend has the same stuffed bear!

B. Write the word in ( ) correctly to show belonging.

1. The _____ shoe is untied. (boy)

2. _____ scarf is on the floor. (Fran)

3. A button came off of the _____ shirt. (man)

C. Look at the picture. Whose hat blew away? Write a sentence to answer the question.

Put It On

A. Read each sentence. Circle the adjective.

1. Jake puts on green pants.

2. Ann puts on a fuzzy scarf.

3. Ely puts on a long coat.

B. Read each sentence. Look at the adjective. Draw a line to what it tells about.

1. I have a <u>red</u> hat.   how it smells

2. I have a <u>soft</u> shirt.   how it looks

3. I have a <u>stinky</u> sock.   how it feels

C. Draw a picture of something you like to wear. Write two adjectives to tell about it.

Feet Everywhere

A. Look at each picture. Write a word from the word box to tell about the noun.

tall old muddy

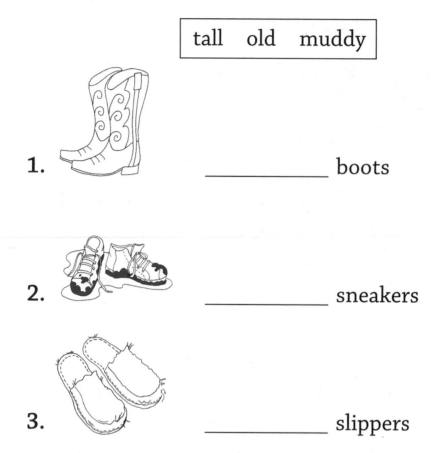

1. _____ boots

2. _____ sneakers

3. _____ slippers

B. Complete each sentence. Use a word from the word box.

big flat tiny

1. A clown has _____ feet.

2. A baby has _____ feet.

3. A duck has _____ feet.

C. Write a sentence about your feet. Use an adjective to describe them.

Yuck!

A. Answer each question. Use a word from the word box.

sticky pink loud sweet

1. Which word tells how something <u>looks</u>?

   _____

2. Which word tells how something <u>sounds</u>?

   _____

3. Which word tells how something <u>feels</u>?

   _____

4. Which word tells how something <u>tastes</u>?

   _____

B. Complete the story. Use words from the word box.

loud sticky new short

Carter had _____ shoes. He went for

a walk. He stepped on some _____ gum.

Then he gave a _____ cry, "Oh no!" It was

a very _____ walk.

C. Draw a picture of something sticky or messy. Write a sentence about it. Use an adjective.

The Happy Elephant

A. Read the story. Circle each article.

Charlie draws an animal. It is an elephant.

It has a long trunk. Charlie draws a smile. The

elephant is happy.

B. Look at the article in front of each noun. Circle the article that is correct.

1. a leg   an leg

2. a arm   an arm

3. an ears   the ears

C. Write a sentence about the picture. Use one of these articles: *a, an,* or *the*. You can use more than one article if you want.

All About Birds

A. Draw a line from each article to the noun that could come after it.

1. a   wings

2. an   beak

3. the   eye

B. Complete each sentence with *A*, *An*, or *The*. Use each word only once.

1. _____ owl is a bird.

2. _____ little birds cannot fly.

3. _____ bird can make a nest.

C. Write a sentence about the birds in the picture. Use *a*, *an*, or *the* in your sentence.

My Parts

A. Look at each noun. Look at the two articles. Write the article that can come before the noun.

1. _____ foot | a   an |

2. _____ ear | a   an |

3. _____ hands | an   the |

4. _____ eyes | the   a |

B. Cross out the sentence that is wrong.

1. A person has two arms.

An person has two arms.

2. An arm has a hand at the end.

A arm has a hand at the end.

3. An ring is on my finger.

The ring is on my finger.

C. Complete the sentences so they tell about the picture.

Here is a _____. He eats an

_____. He holds _____ umbrella.

At the Hat Store

A. Read each sentence. Circle the preposition.

1. We go to the hat store.

2. There is a sale at the store.

3. The store opens in ten minutes.

B. Write the number of the sentence on the line that tells about each picture.

_____ _____ _____

1. The lady walks toward the hats.

2. The hat is on the lady's head.

3. The hat is in the lady's bag.

C. Write a sentence about your favorite thing to wear and how you wear it. Use _in_, _on_, or _at_.

At the Shoe Store

A. Look at the picture. Complete each sentence with a word from the word box.

in	on	at

1. One shoe is _____ the box.

2. One shoe is _____ the man's foot.

3. The man is _____ the shoe store.

B. Complete the story. Use the words from the word box.

in	during	at

The man wears his new shoes _____

the day. He does not wear his shoes _____

night. He wears his socks _____ bed.

C. Write a sentence about your favorite shoes. Tell when you wear them. Where do you go? Use *in*, *on*, *at*, *to*, or *during*.

At the Market

A. Draw a line under the words that tell about each picture.

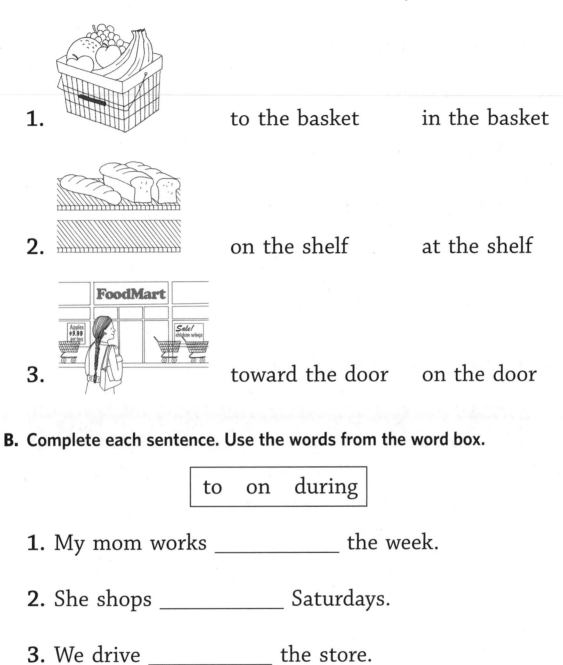

1.   to the basket   in the basket

2.   on the shelf   at the shelf

3.   toward the door   on the door

B. Complete each sentence. Use the words from the word box.

| to   on   during |

1. My mom works _____ the week.

2. She shops _____ Saturdays.

3. We drive _____ the store.

C. Write about going to a store. Use two of these words: *in*, *on*, *at*, and *to*. Draw a picture to go with your writing.

School Rules

A. Read the two sentences. Draw a line under the command.

1. Get out some paper.

I need some paper.

2. Where is your pencil?

Find your pencil, please.

3. The books are on the table.

Please bring me the books.

B. Use the words in the chart to write three commands.

Verbs	Prepositions	Nouns
walk	on	chair
sit	toward	door
eat	at	lunchtime

1. _____

2. _____

3. _____

C. Help someone get from the front of your school to your classroom. Write two commands.

Family Picture

A. Read the story. Circle three mistakes with words that show belonging.

Luke has brown hair. Lukes sister, Lucy, has red hair. Lucy's hair is also curly. Luke hair is straight.

Luke and Lucy have a baby brother. The babys head is bare! He does not have hair yet.

B. Complete the second sentence with the underlined word. Add 's to show belonging.

1. The <u>child</u> has green eyes.

   The _____ eyes are pretty.

2. The <u>lady</u> has long nails.

   The _____ nails are red.

3. The <u>man</u> has a beard.

   The _____ beard is gray.

C. Think of someone in your family. Write a sentence about the person's hair or eyes. Use a noun that shows belonging.

Campfire Fun

A. Complete each sentence. Use a word from the word box.

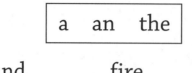

| a | an | the |

1. We sit around _____ fire.

2. I hear _____ sound.

3. _____ owl hoots in a tree.

B. Complete the story. Use adjectives from the word box.

| crunchy | hot | soft |

I put a _____ marshmallow on a stick.

I hold the marshmallow over the _____

fire. The marshmallow burns! I eat it anyway.

I like _____ marshmallows.

C. Write a sentence about the picture. Use *a*, *an*, or *the*. Include an adjective such as *warm*, *cold*, *bright*, or *dark*.

Showtime

A. Read each sentence. Circle the pronoun.

1. I like to dance.

2. You like to sing.

3. We will put on a show.

B. Draw a line from each pronoun to its matching picture.

1. they

2. she

3. he

4. it

C. Write a sentence about one of the pictures on this page. Use *he, she, they,* or *it*.

Get in Line!

A. Look at the picture. Complete each sentence with a word from the word box.

He	She	It

1. _____ is a long line.

2. _____ leads the band.

3. _____ goes last.

B. Look at each picture. Complete each sentence with a word from the word box.

I	We	You

1. _____ am the leader.

2. _____ are too loud!

3. _____ sound good.

C. Write a sentence about one of the pictures on this page. Use the pronoun *they*.

Making Music

A. Circle the pronoun that could replace the underlined word or words.

1. <u>Mom</u> played the piano.   He   She

2. <u>Dad</u> hummed a tune.   He   They

3. <u>The children</u> listened to a song.   They   It

4. <u>The radio</u> was on.   She   It

5. <u>The songs</u> were pretty.   It   They

B. Look at the picture. Complete each sentence with a word from the word box.

I   We   You

1. _____ will put on a show.

2. _____ will play the piano.

3. _____ can sing.

C. Draw a picture of yourself playing an instrument. Write a sentence about the picture. Use the word *I*.

Mouse in the House

A. Read each sentence. Circle the pronoun _I_, _me_, _we_, or _us_.

1. We see a mouse!

2. The mouse runs from us.

3. I look for the mouse.

4. The mouse does not look for me.

B. Look at each picture. Draw a line under the sentence that tells about it.

1.

   I see a mouse.

   We see a mouse.

2.

   The mouse runs from me.

   The mouse runs from us.

C. Pretend you have a pet mouse. Draw a picture of you and your mouse. Write a sentence about it.

Funny Bunny

A. Choose the correct word to complete each sentence.
Write the word on the line.

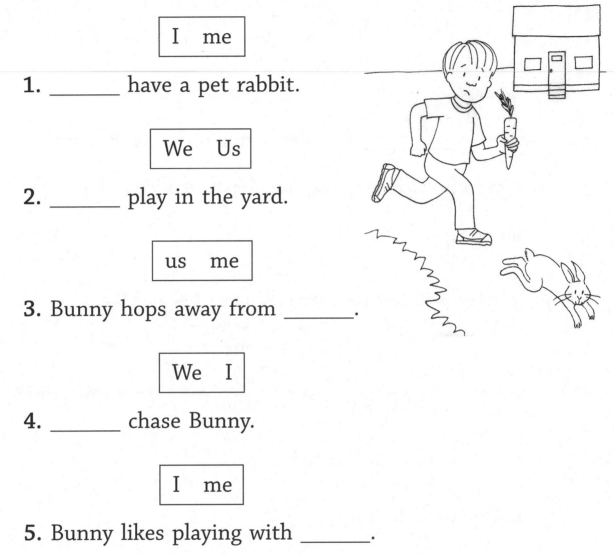

I	me

1. _____ have a pet rabbit.

We	Us

2. _____ play in the yard.

us	me

3. Bunny hops away from _____.

We	I

4. _____ chase Bunny.

I	me

5. Bunny likes playing with _____.

B. Pretend you are a rabbit. Write a sentence about what you do or
where you go.

Let's Get a Pet

A. Read the story. Complete each sentence with a word from the word box.

I	me	us	We

I want a pet. _____ go to the pet store. Dad

takes _____. _____ see a snake. A snake is not

a good pet for me. We see a fish. A fish is a good

pet for _____.

B. Complete each sentence with a word from the word box.

I	We	us

1. _____ feed the fish together.

2. _____ watch the fish.

3. Do the fish see _____?

C. Pretend you are in the fish tank! Write three sentences about what you would do or see.

Snow Day

A. Read each sentence. Circle the pronoun *him*, *her*, *he*, or *she*.

1. She plays in the snow.

2. Freddy plays with her.

3. He slides on the ice.

4. Amy slides with him.

B. Circle the pronoun that can take the place of each underlined noun.

1. <u>Justin</u> makes a snowball.   He   Him

2. Justin gives the snowball to <u>Maria</u>.   she   her

C. Write a sentence about something you do with a friend. Use *him* or *her* in the sentence.

Stuck!

A. Choose the correct word to complete each sentence. Write the word on the line.

He   Him

1. _____ is stuck in the snow.

Her   She

2. _____ helps Mr. Lee.

him   her

3. Mr. Lee thanks _____.

B. Write the pronoun that can take the place of the underlined word or words.

1. The car belongs to <u>the man</u>.   _____

2. <u>The girl</u> digs the car out of the snow.   _____

3. The driver waves to <u>the girl</u>.   _____

C. Write about a time when you helped someone. Use *him* or *her* in your sentence.

At the Rink

A. Complete the story. Use the words from the word box.

He	She	him	her

Tessa skates on the ice. _____ is fast.

She skates faster than Jim does. Tessa passes

_____. _____ speeds up. He catches

up to _____.

B. Complete the story. Use the words from the word box.

He	She	him	her

Mom is a good skater. _____ can spin

and jump. Dad watches _____. Dad cannot

skate. _____ cannot spin or jump. But Mom

will teach _____.

C. Draw someone you know who does something well. Write a sentence about the person. Use *he* or *she*.

Grow, Grow, Grow

A. Read each pair of sentences. Circle the pronoun *they*, *them*, or *it*.

1. The boys dig a hole.

They put seeds in the hole.

2. Flowers grow from the seeds.

The boys water them.

3. One flower grows fast.

It is huge!

B. Circle the pronoun that could replace the underlined words in each sentence.

1. <u>The plants</u> grow tall.   They   Them

2. The boys take care of <u>the plants</u>.   they   them

3. <u>A flower</u> blooms.   It   They

C. Write a sentence about the picture on this page. Use *they* or *it*.

Yummy Fruit

A. Choose the correct word to complete each sentence. Write each word on the line.

They   Them

1. _____ like fruit.

they   them

2. Aunt Jody buys a

   watermelon for _____.

it   them

3. She cuts _____ into pieces.

B. Write the pronoun that can take the place of the underlined words. Use a pronoun from the word box.

it   They   them

1. <u>The children</u> eat the watermelon. _____

2. Aunt Jody eats with <u>the children</u>. _____

3. The family enjoys <u>the watermelon</u>. _____

C. Draw a picture of a fruit you like. Write a sentence about the picture. Use the word *it*.

Poems

A. Read the story. Circle the three pronouns.

The children write a poem. It is called "Friends." They read the poem to Mr. Lam. Mr. Lam likes it!

B. Complete the story with pronouns from the word box.

It	They	them

The children make a poster. _____ write the poem on it. Everyone reads the poem. _____ makes people happy. Other children write a poem. Mr. Lam helps _____. He is proud of his students.

C. Write two sentences about reading a poem or a story to a group. Use _they_ and _them_.

Hidden Rocks

A. Read each sentence. Circle the pronoun that shows belonging: *your*, *her*, or *my*.

1. My sister, Cora, collects rocks.

2. Cora hides her rocks.

3. Mom asks, "Where are your rocks?"

B. Read each sentence. Circle the word that can take the place of the underlined word.

1. Dad looks in <u>Dad's</u> office.   his   your

2. Mom looks in <u>Mom's</u> car.   their   her

3. I find Cora's rocks under <u>Cora's</u> bed.   our   her

C. Write about something you have that you like a lot. Use the word *my*.

Smile!

A. Choose the correct word to complete each sentence. Write each word on the line.

their   his

1. Uncle Manny shows us _____ camera.

your   my

2. He asks, "Can I take _____ picture?"

their   our

3. We want _____ picture taken!

B. Circle the pronoun that completes each sentence. Write each word on the line.

1. The picture belongs to us.

   It is _____ picture.   his   our

2. The camera belongs to you.

   It is _____ camera.   your   my

3. The book belongs to my brothers.

   It is _____ book.   his   their

C. Write a sentence about something that belongs to you. Use the word *my* or *our*.

New Teeth

A. Circle the three pronouns that are wrong.

Deb lost her tooth. Fred lost our tooth, too.

The children put them under my pillows.

Then the teeth were gone. Did the tooth

fairy take my teeth?

B. Complete the story. Use the words from the word box.

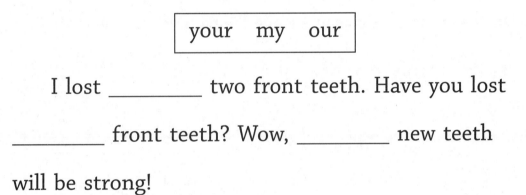

your   my   our

I lost _____ two front teeth. Have you lost

_____ front teeth? Wow, _____ new teeth

will be strong!

C. Write two sentences about the picture. Use the words *his* and *her*.

Eat Your Vegetables

A. Read each sentence. Circle the word that tells which one: *this*, *that*, *these*, or *those*.

1. This tomato is juicy.

2. I want that carrot.

3. These peas are cold.

4. Those peas are hot.

B. Draw a line from each sentence to the picture that goes with it.

1. This bean is big.

2. Those beans are small.

C. Write two sentences about things you see in a kitchen. Use *this* in one sentence. Use *that* in the other sentence.

Fall Fruit

A. Complete each sentence. Use words from the word box.

| this | that | these | those |

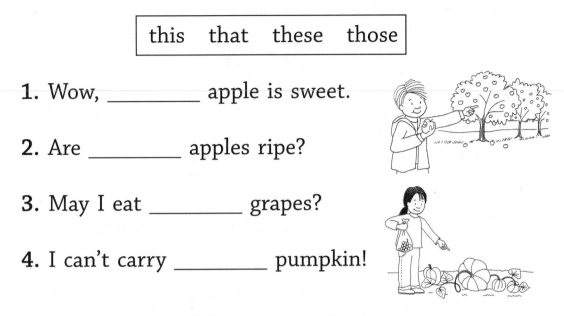

1. Wow, _____ apple is sweet.

2. Are _____ apples ripe?

3. May I eat _____ grapes?

4. I can't carry _____ pumpkin!

B. Write two sentences about the picture. Use *this* in one sentence. Use *these* in the other sentence.

_____

_____

_____

_____

The Zoo

A. Choose the correct word to complete each sentence. Write the word on the line.

| This   These |

1. _____ giraffe takes peanuts from my hand.

| That   Those |

2. _____ monkeys swing on branches.

| This   That |

3. _____ bird sits on the highest branch.

B. Complete each sentence. Use a word from the word box.

| This   These   Those |

1. _____ bear nearby eats fruit.

2. _____ bears are sleeping far from people.

3. _____ cubs play close to us.

C. Pretend you are visiting a zoo. Write two sentences about the animals you see. Use *these* in one sentence and *those* in another sentence.

Party Time

A. Read each sentence. Circle the pronoun *everyone*, *everything*, *anyone*, or *anything*.

1. Anyone can go to the party.

2. Everything is ready.

3. You can wear anything.

4. Everyone has fun.

B. Read each sentence. Draw a line to the picture that goes with it.

1. Everything is on the table.

2. Everyone wears a party hat.

C. Write a sentence about a party game you like to play. Use *everyone* in your sentence.

We Work Together

A. Choose the correct word to complete each sentence. Write the word on the line.

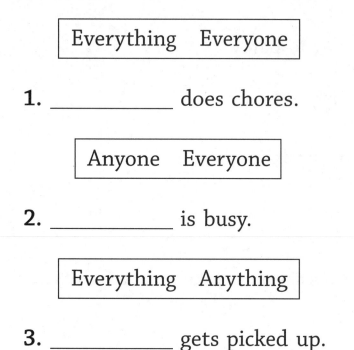

| Everything | Everyone |

1. _____ does chores.

| Anyone | Everyone |

2. _____ is busy.

| Everything | Anything |

3. _____ gets picked up.

B. Complete the sentences with words from the word box. Use one of the words twice.

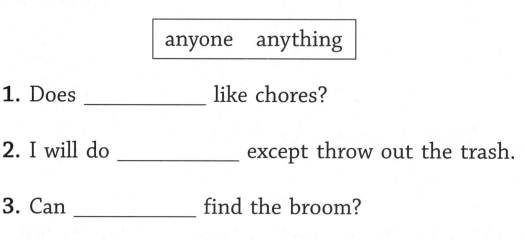

| anyone | anything |

1. Does _____ like chores?

2. I will do _____ except throw out the trash.

3. Can _____ find the broom?

C. Write another sentence about chores. Use *everyone* or *everything* in your sentence.

A Walk in My Neighborhood

A. Choose the correct word to complete each sentence. Write each word on the line.

everything   everyone

1. I wave to _____.

everything   anyone

2. I don't see _____ new.

everyone   anything

3. I know _____ on my street.

B. Complete the story. Use the words from the word box.

anyone   anything   everything

I walk by a pretty house. Does _____

live there? I don't see _____ growing in

the garden. Someone covered _____ on the

porch, too.

C. Write two sentences about your neighborhood. Use *everyone* in one sentence. Use *everything* in the other sentence.

Let's Sing!

A. Read the story. Complete each sentence with a word from the word box.

> | I   me   We   us |

I like to make up songs. _____ will sing

a song for you. Then you can sing a song for

_____. We can make up a song together.

_____ will sound good together!

B. Write the pronoun that can take the place of the underlined noun. Use a pronoun from the word box.

> | He   She   it   him |

1. Grandpa and Grandma sing <u>a song</u>.   _____

2. <u>Grandpa</u> sings the low notes.   _____

3. <u>Grandma</u> sings the high notes.   _____

4. Grandma loves to sing with <u>Grandpa</u>.   _____

C. Write two sentences about singing to a group. Use *they* in one of your sentences.

Let's Paint a Picture

A. Complete the story. Use the words from the word box.

his   her   their

Kenny has a sister named Penny. Kenny paints

a picture of _____ sister. Then Penny paints a

picture of _____ brother. The children look at

_____ pictures. The pictures look alike!

B. Circle the pronoun that completes each sentence.

1. I have blue paint.

It is (your, my) paint.

2. You have yellow paint.

It is (my, your) paint.

3. We make green paint together.

It is (my, our) paint.

C. Draw a picture of someone in your family. Write a sentence about the person. Use *my*, *his*, or *her*.

Let's Build a Fort

A. Choose the correct word to complete each sentence. Write the word on the line.

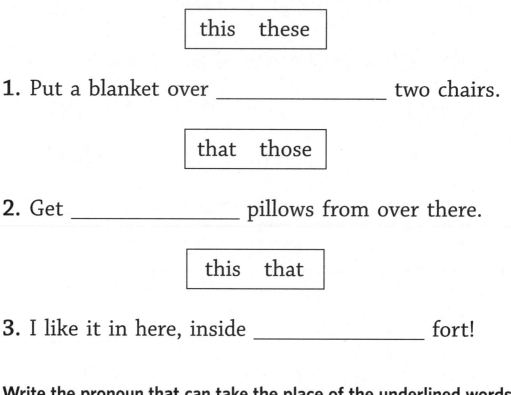

| this   these |

1. Put a blanket over _____ two chairs.

| that   those |

2. Get _____ pillows from over there.

| this   that |

3. I like it in here, inside _____ fort!

B. Write the pronoun that can take the place of the underlined words. Use a pronoun from the word box.

| anyone   everything   everyone |

1. We bring <u>all of our things</u> into the fort.

_____

2. We invite <u>all of our friends</u> into the fort.

_____

3. There is no more room for <u>even one person</u>.

_____

C. Write a sentence about everything you would put in a fort.

School Days

A. Circle the capital letters in the days of the week.

1. The school bake sale is Monday.

2. Mom and I will bake bread on Sunday.

3. The last day of school is Friday.

B. Circle the comma between the day of the month and the year.

1. School will start on September 6, 2016.

2. We will have the Fall Festival on October 15, 2016.

3. Thanksgiving is on November 24, 2016.

C. Draw a picture of your favorite school holiday. Write its date below the picture.

All Around the Year

A. Answer each question. Write the name of the day.

1. What day comes after Sunday? _____

2. What day comes after Thursday? _____

3. What day comes before Sunday? _____

B. Write the name of the month to complete each sentence.

1. _____ comes after March.

2. _____ comes after June.

3. _____ comes after November.

C. Write the name of your favorite month of the year. Draw a picture of something that happens during that month.

Remember the Date

A. **What's missing from each date? Write the dates correctly on the lines.**

1. October 12 2016

   _____

2. July 4 2017

   _____

3. November 24 2018

   _____

B. **Write the date on the line to complete each sentence.**

1. My birthday is

   _____.

2. One classmate's birthday is

   _____.

3. My best friend's birthday is

   _____.

C. **Draw a picture of a family member. Write that person's name and birth date below the picture.**

Summertime Fun!

A. Circle the commas that separate the things in a list.

1. Nahla can wade, swim, and dive in the pool.

2. Sasha, Matt, and Lauren watch the swimmers.

3. We bring tubes, rafts, and kickboards into the water.

B. Add commas where they are needed in each list.

1. We hike to the meadow the pond and the forest.

2. Matt sees a frog a fish and a dragonfly.

3. Lauren sees daisies dandelions and buttercups.

C. Write a sentence that lists three things you can see outside.

Nature Walk

A. Look at the picture. Write a sentence that tells three things you see. Use commas to separate the things.

bushes

pond

flowers

frog

children

butterflies

berries

_____

_____

_____

B. What are three things you will do this summer? Write them in a sentence. Add commas to separate the things.

_____

_____

_____

Cooking Fun

A. Proofread the sentences. Add any missing commas between items in a series.

Nadia Jonah and Clare took a cooking class last summer. They made pancakes muffins and applesauce. Their teacher showed them how to blend stir and mash.

B. Pick three things to put on a pizza. Then write a sentence that tells what you picked.

meatballs   chicken   mushrooms
peppers   extra sauce

_____

_____

_____

C. What would you like to learn how to cook? Write a sentence listing three foods. Use commas to separate the foods.

The Children's Zoo

A. Read each compound sentence. Circle the comma and the word *and*, *or*, or *but*.

1. Ling loves animals, and she visits the children's zoo.

2. Roy wanted to go, but he got sick.

3. Ling can pet the goats, or she can feed the ducks.

B. Complete each sentence. Add a comma and a word from the word box.

and   or   but

1. Ling rides a pony _____ she brushes a cow.

2. She finds the bunnies _____ she can't find the sheep.

3. Ling can ride the zoo train _____ she can walk on the path.

C. Write a compound sentence that tells about the pictures.

A Visit to the Firehouse

A. Complete each compound sentence. Add a comma and a word from the word box.

| and | or | but |

1. The children visit the firehouse _____ they have fun.

2. They stand on a truck _____ they do not ride on it.

3. They can ring a bell _____ they can watch other kids ring it.

4. The children want to stay _____ it is time to leave.

5. The kids walk home _____ they take the bus.

B. Draw a picture of a fire truck and a firefighter. Write a compound sentence about your picture.

Fun at the Fair

A. Read the story. Draw a line under the two compound sentences.

The kids love the fair. Nate rides the merry-go-round, and Coco plays a game. They eat popcorn. Nate gets a balloon, but it blows away. Coco gives Nate her balloon.

B. Use *and, or,* or *but* to join the sentences. Write the new sentences on the lines.

1. Nate plays a game. He wins a prize.

   _____

   _____

2. The children can play more games. They can get a snack.

   _____

   _____

3. The fair is almost over. The children are not tired.

   _____

   _____

C. Write a compound sentence that tells about something fun you did.

What Day Is It?

A. Read each sentence. Write the missing letter to complete the name of the day.

1. The first day of the school week is ___onday.

2. The day after Thursday is ___riday.

3. Saturday comes before ___unday.

B. Rewrite each date correctly.

1. july 7, 2016

   _____

2. May 25 2016

   _____

3. december, 18, 2017

   _____

C. What is your favorite day of the week? Write a sentence that tells why it is your favorite day.

Fly, Swim, and Crawl

A. Read each sentence. Add commas where they belong.

1. A bird has wings feathers and a beak.

2. Birds eat seeds bugs and worms.

3. I saw a bird sing hop and fly away.

4. Robins crows and jays are three kinds of birds.

B. Complete each sentence using all the words in the word box. Add commas and the word *and*.

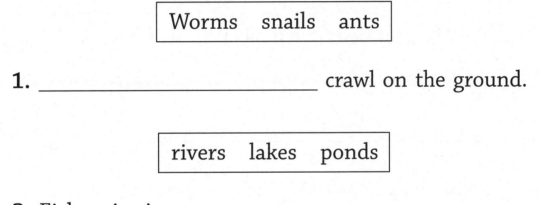

Worms   snails   ants

1. _____ crawl on the ground.

rivers   lakes   ponds

2. Fish swim in _____.

C. Think of your favorite animal. Write a sentence that lists three things it can do. Add commas where they belong.

Sleepy Time

A. Complete each sentence with a comma and a word from the word box. Use each word once.

| and or but |

1. I feel tired _____ I want to go to sleep.

2. I try to sleep _____ the baby keeps me awake.

3. I will stay in my bed _____ I will get Dad.

B. Write each pair of sentences as a compound sentence. Add a comma before *and*, *or*, or *but*.

1. We sleep in beds. Fish sleep in water.

   _____ but

   _____

2. Seals sleep on rocks. They sleep on sand.

   _____ or

   _____

3. Bats sleep in caves. They eat at night.

   _____ and

   _____

C. What are two things you do to get ready for bed? Write a compound sentence about them.

Student Grammar Guide

Sentences

A **sentence** has a <u>naming part</u> and a <u>telling part</u>.
It begins with a **capital letter**.

<u>**T**he teacher</u> <u>reads a story</u>.

There are different kinds of sentences.

- A **telling sentence** tells about something. It ends with a **period**.

  The book is on the desk.

- A **question** asks something. It ends with a **question mark**.

  Do you have my book?

- A **command** tells someone what to do. It usually ends with a **period**.

  Please bring me that book.

- Some sentences show **strong feeling**. They end with an **exclamation point**.

  This is a great story!

You can join two sentences to make a **compound sentence**. Use a **comma** and the word **and**, **but**, or **or**.

We like to play inside, <u>and</u> we like to play outside.

We can play inside, <u>or</u> we can play outside.

Today we played inside, <u>but</u> we did not play outside.

Nouns

A **noun** names a person, a place, or a thing. It can also name an animal, such as a cat or a bird.

Person	Place	Thing
boy	school	balloon
girl	park	cap
coach	store	glass

A noun can tell about **one** or **more than one**.

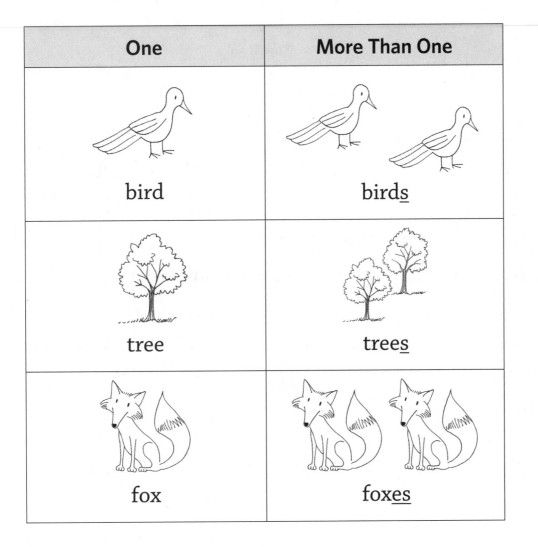

One	More Than One
bird	bird<u>s</u>
tree	tree<u>s</u>
fox	fox<u>es</u>

(continues)

Nouns *(continued)*

A **proper noun** names a special person, place, animal, or thing. It begins with a **capital letter**.

Nick

Central Park

Buddy

A noun can show **belonging**, or what someone or something has. It ends with an **apostrophe** and *s*.

the dog's bowl

the spider's web

the boy's umbrella

Verbs

A **verb** is an **action word** that tells what someone or something does.

swim	ride	paint
read	eat	sleep
kick	hop	run
jump	swing	talk

(continues)

Verbs (continued)

A verb can tell when an action happens.

- A verb can tell about an action happening **now**.

  Today Dad <u>cooks</u>.

- A verb can tell about an action that happened **in the past**.

  Yesterday Mom <u>cooked</u>.

- A verb can tell about an action that will happen **in the future**.

  Tomorrow I <u>will cook</u>.

A verb must match the noun it tells about.

One	More Than One
 One hen <u>clucks</u>.	 Two hens <u>cluck</u>.

Adjectives

An **adjective** can tell how something **looks**, **feels**, **tastes**, **smells**, or **sounds**.

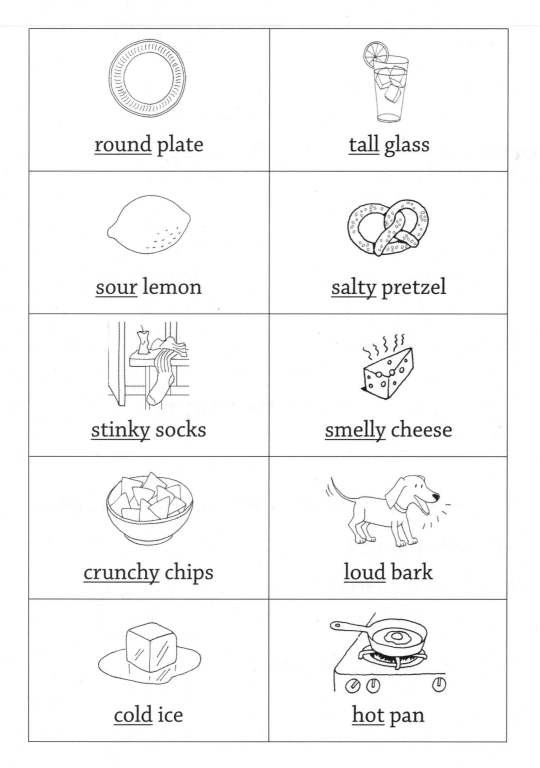

round plate	tall glass
sour lemon	salty pretzel
stinky socks	smelly cheese
crunchy chips	loud bark
cold ice	hot pan

Prepositions

A **preposition** is a short word that can help tell **where** something is.

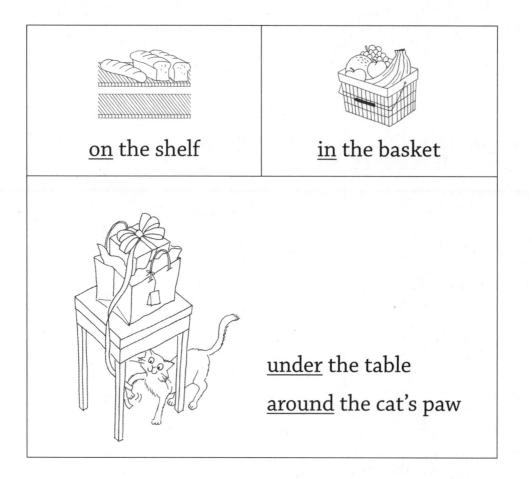

on the shelf

in the basket

under the table

around the cat's paw

A preposition can also help tell **when** something happens.

We will leave in six days.

We always eat dinner at 6:00.

I will see you on Friday.

The baby naps during the day.

Pronouns

A **pronoun** is a word that can take the place of a noun.

He drums.

She blows the horn.

It is loud.

They are loud.

I like to sing.

You sing well.

We both like to sing.

He likes how we sing.

(continues)

Pronouns *(continued)*

Some pronouns do not tell about a specific person or thing.

Everyone is at the museum.

I see everything.

Anyone can go to the museum.

I can't see anything.

Some pronouns come after a verb or a preposition.

Grandma helps <u>him</u>.

Grandpa helps <u>them</u>.

Throw <u>me</u> the ball.

I will throw it back to <u>you</u>.

This is a good game for <u>us</u>.

(continues)

Pronouns *(continued)*

Some pronouns show **belonging**.

	<u>his</u> hamster
	<u>her</u> lizard
	<u>their</u> bird
	<u>our</u> pup
	<u>my</u> snake
	<u>your</u> rabbit

Articles *A*, *An*, and *The*

Use **a** and **an** when you talk about **one general** thing.

Use *a* before a consonant.

I see <u>a</u> bird.

Use *an* before a vowel.

I see <u>an</u> elephant.

Use **the** to talk about **one** or **more than one specific** thing. You can use *the* before a consonant or a vowel.

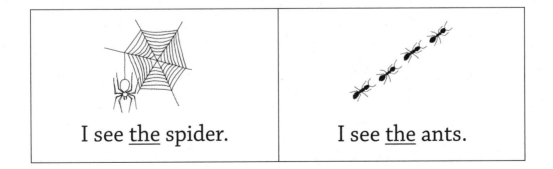

I see <u>the</u> spider.　　　I see <u>the</u> ants.

This, That, These, and Those

Use **this** to talk about **one** thing **near** you. Use **that** to talk about **one** thing **farther** away.

this book   that book

Use **these** to talk about **more than one** thing **near** you. Use **those** to talk about **more than one** thing **farther** away.

these crayons   those crayons

Days and Dates

The days of the week begin with a **capital letter**.

<u>S</u>unday <u>M</u>onday <u>T</u>uesday <u>W</u>ednesday

<u>T</u>hursday <u>F</u>riday <u>S</u>aturday

When you write the date, put a **comma** between the day and the year.

July 4, 2015   December 31, 1999

Commas in a List

Use a **comma** to separate words in a list.

I play soccer on Monday, Thursday, and Saturday.

Jim, Kaleb, and Ruby are on my team.

Tasks

Task 1

Draw a line under the correct word or words to complete each sentence.

1. I ride my bike to my _____ house.

   a. friend

   b. friends

   c. friend's

2. I _____ about ten hours every night.

   a. sleep

   b. sleeps

   c. sleeping

3. Susan _____ her dog every afternoon.

   a. walk

   b. walks

   c. walking

4. My brother Juan fixes _____ own lunch.

   a. his

   b. her

   c. him

5. The children take care of _____ own kitten.

   a. her

   b. their

   c. your

6. Tomorrow we _____ a special dinner.

   a. cook

   b. cooked

   c. will cook

7. Now I _____ some juice.

   a. want

   b. wanted

   c. will want

8. The lake looks _____ today.

   a. noisy

   b. green

   c. sour

9. The ice cube feels _____.

   a. cold

   b. sweet

   c. tall

GO ON →

10. I like cherries, _____ I like grapes more.

    a. or

    b. and

    c. but

11. Dad left the beach, _____ Ben went with him.

    a. or

    b. but

    c. and

12. _____ pencil is mine.

    a. This

    b. These

    c. Those

13. _____ kittens play with the yarn.

    a. A

    b. The

    c. An

14. The ship sailed _____ the ocean.

    a. under

    b. above

    c. across

15. My dog sleeps _____ his own bed.

  a. in

  b. during

  c. over

Read each question and draw a line under the correct answer.

16. Which word should begin with a capital letter?

> My best friend lives in a city called oakland.

  a. friend

  b. city

  c. oakland

17. Which is the best way to make these two sentences into one sentence?

> Sam can keep the dime.
> He can spend it.

  a. Sam can keep the dime, or he can spend it.

  b. Sam can keep the dime or he can spend it.

  c. Sam can keep the dime, he can spend it.

GO ON ➤

18. Which is the best way to make these two sentences into one sentence?

> I know where my socks are.
> I can't find my shoes.

   a. I know where my socks are or I can't find my shoes.

   b. I know where my shoes or socks are.

   c. I know where my socks are, but I can't find my shoes.

19. Which sentence is written correctly?

   a. Fran was born on May 10 2007.

   b. Fran was born on May, 10 2007.

   c. Fran was born on May 10, 2007.

20. Which sentence is written correctly?

   a. We grew peas corn and lettuce.

   b. We grew peas, corn, and lettuce.

   c. We grew peas, corn and, lettuce.

Write the words in each box as a sentence. Use capital letters and end punctuation where they are needed.

21. | My birthday is in june |

_____

_____

22. | Is sara your sister |

_____

_____

Task 2

Draw a line under the correct word or words to complete each sentence.

1. My little _____ bike is purple.

   a. sister

   b. sisters'

   c. sister's

2. Jess _____ really good bread.

   a. bake

   b. bakes

   c. baking

3. I _____ to my grandmother every week.

   a. talk

   b. talks

   c. talking

4. My sister can stand on _____ head.

   a. his

   b. her

   c. hers

5. Who gave this to _____?

   a. you

   b. your

   c. yours

6. Yesterday we _____ a funny movie.

   a. watch

   b. watched

   c. will watch

7. Tomorrow Ken _____ his cousin.

   a. visit

   b. visited

   c. will visit

8. The sun is very _____ today.

   a. hot

   b. soft

   c. green

9. The new car is very _____.

   a. sour

   b. shiny

   c. scratchy

10. I went to his house, _____ he was not at home.

   a. or

   b. so

   c. but

11. I can rent the red bike, _____ I can buy the blue one.

   a. so

   b. because

   c. or

12. _____ children over there are going to lunch.

   a. Those

   b. These

   c. That

13. I found _____ dollar bill on the sidewalk.

   a. a

   b. an

   c. those

14. I sat _____ the tree to rest.

    a. above

    b. under

    c. through

15. I will give this hat _____ my sister.

    a. in

    b. to

    c. from

Read each question and draw a line under the correct answer.

16. Which word in this sentence should begin with a capital letter?

> My cousin lives in boston.

    a. cousin

    b. in

    c. boston

GO ON

17. Which is the best way to make these two sentences into one sentence?

> I like beans.
> I do not like peas.

a. Beans I like peas I do not like.

b. I like beans, but I do not like peas.

c. I like beans, and peas.

18. Which is the best way to make these two sentences into one sentence?

> We can play at your house.
> We can go to my house.

a. We can play at your house but not at my house.

b. We can play at your house, but we can go to my house.

c. We can play at your house, or we can go to my house.

Read each question and draw a line under the correct answer.

19. Which sentence is written correctly?

    a. I was born on June 12, 2008.

    b. I was born on June, 12 2008.

    c. I was born on June 12 2008.

20. Which sentence is written correctly?

    a. We ate bread cheese and fruit on our picnic.

    b. We ate bread cheese, and fruit on our picnic.

    c. We ate bread, cheese, and fruit on our picnic.

Write the words in the box as a sentence. Use capital letters and end punctuation where they are needed.

21. | My   friend   tim   likes soccer |

_____

_____

22. | Is   soccer   on   Monday |

_____

_____

STOP